Monographic Journals of the Near East
General Editor: Giorgio Buccellati

Assur

Volume 1

Issue 3

August 1974

A. Leo Oppenheim, 1904 - 1974

Notes on Some Nineveh Horse Lists

by

Frederick Mario Fales

Undena Publications

Malibu 1974

ASSUR

ASSUR is meant to serve the needs of the specialized field which is closely identified with the study of Assyrian as a dialect of Akkadian and with the history of Assyria as a special aspect of Mesopotamian civilization, from early times down to the end of the Assyrian empire. Given the intensity of linguistic and historical exchanges with neighboring regions, it is clear that the study of Assyrian dialect and history cannot be carried on in isolation, without due consideration to influences deriving from contacts with other people. Hence, ASSUR will also accept articles which are not exclusively Assyrian in scope, as long as they are related to Assyria and useful for the study of its language and history.

(Address correspondence to Dr. C. Saporetti, Via Vasanello 20, Cassia, 00189 Roma, Italy)

Volume 1

Issue 1: S. Parpola, *The Alleged Middle/Neo-Assyrian Irregular Verb *naṣṣ and the Assyrian Sound Change /š/ > /s/*

Forms of the alleged irregular and defective verb **naṣṣ*, reconstructed as occurring in Middle and Neo-Assyrian texts, are in fact to be understood as forms of the verb *našû*–and hence **naṣṣ* is to be stricken from the dictionaries. The argumentation is based on five considerations. (1) Forms assigned to *našû* and **naṣṣ* respectively are in perfect complementary distribution: missing forms of *našû* are covered by **naṣṣ* and vice versa. (2) Semantically, both verbs are used in exactly the same function. (3) The paradigm is morphologically perfect in the sense that all forms of **naṣṣ* conform to the paradigm of *našû* as known from the Old Assyrian period (in which no forms of **naṣṣ* are attested). (4) There is firm evidence for the validity of the change /*š*/ > /*s*/ in the phonological system of Neo-Assyrian. (5) Writings with <*ṣa*> and <*ṣu*> stand for phonemic /*ssa*/ and /*ssu*/.

Issue 2: C. Saporetti, *Some Considerations on the Stelae of Assur*

The publication of new texts has led to the identification of some of the eponyms mentioned in the steles of Assur. An analysis of the data results in a negative conclusion with regard to the possibility of arranging the steles in groups characterized by internal chronological coherence. The original sequence has been lost, and even within the same group there are steles dated to disparate periods, even if they are all Middle-Assyrian. Possibly, a subdivision may be suggested between the steles placed to the North, which may be rather late, and those placed to the South, which may be dated to the period of greatest power–but this differentiation might be accidental.

A. Leo Oppenheim

1904-1974

Just at the start of the new life and academic surroundings that his retirement in Berkeley had brought him, Professor Leo Oppenheim, in his seventieth year, was vigorously looking forward to the accomplishment of many Assyriological projects, and the full enjoyment of life in California together with his wife, Elizabeth. For us, at the University of California, his sudden death on July 21 meant that we were deprived of a close friend, and that we could no longer eagerly anticipate the many years of benefiting from his presence. Our sense of loss is perhaps especially great because Professor Oppenheim was, until the moment of the unexpected heart attack that took him from us, still very much in the prime of his academic life.

During the forty years since receiving his doctorate in Assyriology in 1933 from the University of Vienna, Professor Oppenheim's talents and energies were channeled into his studies which led to significant contributions concerning the civilization of ancient Mesopotamia and its neighbors. Though his career was seriously interrupted by the wartime situation between 1938 and 1940, which years he spent in France, he very quickly began to produce many impressive articles (for an eventual total of more than one hundred) and books (seven, in addition to the Chicago Assyrian Dictionary which he edited) after his arrival in the United States in 1941.

Between 1941 and 1947, Professor Oppenheim was associated with New York's Asia Institute, Johns Hopkins University, and the Dropsie College of Philadelphia. A major text edition of the economic texts of the Ur III period resulted from his studies of the Wilberforce Eames Babylonian Collection of the New York Public Library. After his call to Chicago's Oriental Institute in 1947, his enormous energies eventually produced the myriad major Assyriological contributions that have become standard works in the field. In 1954 he became Editor-in-Chief of the monumental Chicago Assyrian Dictionary project. In 1966 a first volume of the series, Texts from Cuneiform Sources, was published; Professor Oppenheim initiated this important new series and was its guiding spirit as well as its editor-in-chief. In 1969 he was made the first John A. Wilson Professor of the Oriental Institute. His versatility in the field was extraordinary, his topics having ranged from conchology to dreams, to glassmaking. He was working on a new edition of his best known book, Ancient Mesopotamia: Portrait of a Dead Civilization, when he died. In 1966 this book received the Gordon J. Laing prize from the University of Chicago Press. Another major work, the re-edition of the Late Assyrian and Babylonian astrological reports, was also well underway.

While he was Professor Emeritus at the University of Chicago since 1973, Professor Oppenheim continued his association with the Chicago Assyrian Dictionary project, having spent several months in the fall of 1973 and the spring of 1974 at the Oriental Institute--an arrangement *that was expected to continue. At the University of California in Berkeley, Professor Oppenheim was appointed as Visiting Professor in 1969, and as Visiting Scholar since 1973. In 1971 he was named a corresponding member of the British Academy.*

The impact of Leo Oppenheim's thought on the work of his fellow scholars and students was invariably forceful and provocative. Whenever one came in touch with him, whether in person or through his writings, it was inevitable that one should reflect not only on the specific points he raised, but also on his overall approach to the data. In this sense he has been, and will continue to be through his far-reaching influence, a true teacher in the deep sense of the word–for he has helped shape a mode of thinking, a creative attitude toward the evidence, and a critical stance in front of the scholar as a craftsman. This ideal he himself embodied to the fullest degree–"il miglior fabbro" himself, as in the dedication he thoughtfully chose at one time for Benno Landsberger. He was concrete to the extreme, a superb philologist with a sure command of the minutest details. And yet he had a truly holistic understanding of culture: he had explored countless byways to reach an ever surer grasp of his field, becoming more and more interested in such disciplines as anthropology and the history of technology. In so doing he would constantly take distance from himself and his object of study, in order to gain a dispassionate perspective of what his research was all about–hence his youthful impatience with standard modules, his marvellous irreverence for the banal, however hallowed by tradition, his ironical sense of delight in self-contradiction when useful for heuristic purposes, and his fervid search through whatever avenues seemed to have a promise in store. Some of his text editions are a model in this respect, especially the ones on Dreams and on Glass-making–uncompromising in terms of philological exactness and completeness, and thoroughly innovative in terms of the presentation of the material.

His scholarly legacy and his inspiration will continue to touch us all. It is embodied in the research he had completed or had in progress. It is embodied in the work of his students and research associates, so many of whom are now working in most major North-American institutions and (especially through the association with the Chicago Assyrian Dictionary) in Europe as well.

Though we have not spoken of the overwhelming sense of personal loss that is felt–for he was well-loved by the present writers–it is a sad reality that we are left with a great emptiness. It is impossible to capture his spirit in a few words–nor in a larger critical assessment, for that matter. That is why his loss, to us friends and fellow Assyriologists, is truly and finally irreparable.

Anne Draffkorn Kilmer
University of California, Berkeley

Giorgio Buccellati
University of California, Los Angeles

NOTES ON SOME NINEVEH HORSE LISTS[1]

Frederick Mario Fales

Rome, Italy

The article contains new documentary evidence on horses in Neo-Assyrian times, including the copies, transliterations and translations of three hitherto unpublished and four other texts from Nineveh. The discussion of the data provides an analysis of the internal structure and the nature of the texts. In one group, the horses are classified according to their color, sex and (possibly) age; these texts probably represent the preliminary listing of incoming animals, drawn up for internal use by the administrative unit of the palace in charge of horses. Another group consists of memoranda on specific quantities of horses, which are reports sent daily to the king by the same administrative unit, to provide an "ephemeral" (i.e. not destined to archival files) account of events.

1. An unpublished text on the color of horses.

A. Rm. 949 (= Fig. 1).

Obv. * 1. ⌜*4*?⌝ ⌜KUR ^{MÍ}ḪÚB⌝ ^{MEŠ}

2. PAP *6* KUR^{MEŠ} ^{I}EN.K⌜I⌝-[x]

3. ŠU^{II} ^{I}DÙ-*ia* [( )]

---

4. *1* KUR *ir-gi-n*[*u* *2* K]UR ^{MÍ}ḪÚB^{MEŠ}

Lower edge 1. [PAP] *3* KUR^{MEŠ} ^{I}*Ḫar-ma*-[x x]

---

1 The present article has been written in the general framework of studies on Ancient Near Eastern techniques, financed by the Italian Consiglio Nazionale delle Ricerche and conducted by the Centro per le Antichità e la Storia dell' Arte del Vicino Oriente of Rome. The texts are all kept in the Department of Western Asiatic Antiquities of the British Museum; I am grateful to Drs. R. D. Barnett and E. Sollberger for their kind permission to publish the documents. I am also grateful to Profs. Aaron Shaffer and Karlheinz Deller for their kind assistance and suggestions.

2. *1* SA$_5$ 2 KUR GÍG^{MEŠ} [( )]

3. *1* KUR ^{MÍ}ḪÚB^{MEŠ} (!) [( )]

4. PAP 4 ^{I}EN-x [x]

Rev. 1. *2* KUR SA$_5$ *2* KUR *ir-*[*gi-ni/nu*]

2. *2* KUR G[ÍG] ⌞ ^{MEŠ} ⌟ [( )]

3. *2* KUR ^{MÍ}ḪÚB^{MEŠ} [( )]

4. PAP *8* KUR ^{I}x[x x]

---

5. *1* KUR *ir-g*[*i-ni/nu*]

6. [*n*] KUR [x x x x]

(remainder lost)

Transl.: (*Obv.*) "Four mares, a total of six horses of Bēl-isse-[ ], in the hands of Bāniia. One *irginu*-colored horse, two mares (*low. edge*), a total of three horses of Ḫarma-[ ]. One red (horse), two black horses, one mare (!), a total of four (horses) of Bēl-?[ ]. (*Rev.*) Two red horses, two *irginu*-colored horses, two black horses, two mares, a total of eight horses of ? [ ]. One *irginu*-colored horse, *n* horses [ ]" (remainder lost).

This fragment (4, 3 x 3, 6 cms.), in itself hardly remarkable, represents in fact a further example of a particular type of horse list, already attested at Nineveh in three admistrative documents (*ADD* 988, 989, 1103) and in a letter-tablet (*ABL* 466) which shows also contacts with the administrative *genre* of Ninevite text-writing. A check on this material convinced me of the need for new copies of *ADD* 988 and 989 (cf. Figs 2 and 3) and for a collation of the third Johns text; transliterations of all three follow, prior to a discussion on the entire group of tablets.

B. K. 952 = *ADD* 988 (= Fig. 2).

Obv. 1. *6* KUR GÍG^{MEŠ} *2* [+*n* KUR SA$_5$^{MEŠ} (?)]

2. *2* KUR *ir-gi-*[*ni* x x x]

3. *5* KUR ^{MÍ}ḪUB^{MEŠ}

4. PAP 17 KUR^{MEŠ}

5. ^{I}*Ia-ḫu-ṭu*

---

6. *5* KUR GÍG^{MEŠ} *5* KUR *ir-*[*gi-ni*]

7. *2* KUR SA$_5$^{MEŠ} *4* KUR ^{MÍ}ḪÚB$^{\text{M[EŠ]}}$

---

8. [P] AP *16* KUR^{MEŠ} *ša* ^{I}DUMU . XV

9. [*n*] KUR *ir-gi-ni*

10. [*n*] KUR SA$_5$ *6* KUR GÍG^{MEŠ}

11. [*n*] KUR *ḫar-ba-ka-nu*

12. [*n*] KUR *ḫar-ša-a-a*

13. [*n* +] *2* KUR ^{MÍ}ḪÚB^{MEŠ}

14. [PAP] *26* KUR ^{I}EN . DÙ

---

15. [*n* KU] R SA$_5$ *2* KUR ⌞ *ir-gi-ni* ⌟

16. [*n* KUR G] ÍG *9* K[UR ^{MÍ}ḪÚB^{MEŠ}]

17. [PAP *n* +] *2* KUR ^{I}x x[x x x]

Lower edge 1. [PAP-*ma*(?) *n* + (?)] *2* KUR [

2. [ŠU^{II} (?) ^{I}] DÙ-*ia* [

3. [

Rev. (one or two lines missing)

*1. [*n* KUR] GÍG^{MEŠ} *5* KUR [SA$_5$^{MEŠ} (?)]

2. [*n* K] UR *ir-g*[*i-ni* *n* KUR ^{MÍ}ḪÚB^{MEŠ}(?)]

3. [PAP *n* +] *2* KUR^{MEŠ} $^{\text{I.d}}$x [x x]

---

4. [*n* KUR S] A$_5$$^{?}$ 4 *ir-gi-ni*

5. [*n* KUR ^{MÍ}] ḪÚB^{MEŠ} PAP *26* ⌜KUR⌝^{MEŠ}

6. [^{I}(x) x] *-du* ŠU^{II} ^{I}DÙ-*ia*

---

7. [*n* KUR G] ÍG^{MEŠ} *4* SA$_5$ [x x]

8. [*n* K]UR *ir-gi-ni* [x x x x]

9. *2* KUR ^{MÍ}ḪÚ[B^{MEŠ} PAP *n* KUR^{MEŠ} x x]

---

10. *4* KUR *ir-*[*gi-ni* *n* KUR SA$_5$ (?)]

11. *9* KUR GÍ[G^{MEŠ} *n* KUR ^{MÍ}ḪÚB^{MEŠ}]

12. PAP *18* [KUR^{MEŠ} *š*]*a* ^{I}E[N- x x]

---

13. *5* " SA$_5$ ⌞*5*?⌟ " GÍG^{MEŠ} *5* " [*ir-gi-ni* (?)]

14. *1* " *ḫ*[*ar-ša*]*-a-a* 9 KUR ^{MÍ}Ḫ[ÚB^{MEŠ}]

15. PAP [*25* KUR^{MEŠ} (*ša*?) ^{I}]*Ḫar-m*[*a-* x]

---

16. *6* " [GÍG(?)]$^{\text{M[EŠ}}$ *n* "] ⌞*ir-gi*⌟*-ni*

17. *1* " S[A$_5$ *n* " *ḫar-ša-a*]*-a* *5* " ^{MÍ}ḪÚB^{MEŠ}

18. PAP *17* [KUR^{MEŠ} (*ša*?) ^{I}PA]P.AŠ

---

19. *3* KUR [x x x]^{MEŠ} ⌞*u*? S⌟ A$_5$^{MEŠ}

20. *15* KUR ^{MÍ}⌞ḪÚB⌟^{MEŠ}

21. PAP *18* KUR^{MEŠ} ^{I}*A-*⌜*ba*?⌝*-*[x]*-i*

Transl.: (*Obv.*) "Six black horses, 2 + *n* red horses (?), two *irginu*-colored horses, five mares, a total of 17 horses of Iaḫuṭu. Five black horses, five *irginu*-colored horses, two red horses, four mares, a total of 18 horses of Mār-Ištar. *n irginu*-colored horses, *n* red horses, six black horses, *n ḫarbakanu*-colored horses, *n ḫaršāju* horses, *n* + 2 mares, a total of 26 horses of **Bēl-ibni.** *n* red horses, two *irginu*-colored horses, *n* black horses, nine mares, a total of *n* + 2 horses of ?? [ ]. (*lower edge*) A grand total (?) of *n* + 2 horses [ ], in the hands of (?) Bāniia. [ ]. (*Rev.*) (one or two lines missing) *n* black horses, five red horses (?), *n irginu*-colored horses, *n* mares (?), a total of *n* + 2 horses of ? [ ]. *n* red horses, four *irginu*-colored (horses), *n* mares, a total of 26 horses of [ ] du, in the hands of Bāniia. *n* black horses, four red (horses), *n irginu*-colored horses [ ], two mares, a total of *n* horses of [ ]. Four *irginu*-colored horses, *n* red horses (?), nine black horses, *n* mares, a total of 18 horses of Bēl- [ ]. Five red same, five black same, five *irginu*-colored (?) same, one *ḫaršāju* same, nine mares, a total of 25 horses of Ḫarma-[ ]. Six black (?)

same, *n irginu*-colored same, one red same, *n ḫaršāju* same, five mares of same, a total of 17 horses of Aḫu-iddina. Three [ ] horses and (?) red (ones), fifteen mares, a total of 18 horses of Aba? [ ] i.

Notes. Reverse, *1-3: these lines are left blank in Johns' copy in *ADD* II, p. 225.

C. K. 968 = *ADD* 989 (= Fig. 3)

Obv. 1. [x x x x x] x *ša* É.GAL

2. [x x x x *n* +]*3* KUR *ir-gi-* ⸢*ni*⸣

3. [x x x x *n* K]UR *ḫar-ša-a-*[*a*]

4. ⸢*6*? ^{MÍ}ḪÚB KUR^{MEŠ}⸣ [PAP *n* +]*1* KUR$^{M[EŠ]}$

5. [x x] x x [x x x x x]

6. [*n*] KUR [x x] *1* KUR [x x x]

7. [*n*] KUR [x x x x x x x]

8. [*n*] KUR [x x x x x x x]

9. [*n*] KUR GÍ[G x x x x x x]

(ll. 10-14 totally lost)

15. [x x x x x x x *n*] KUR SA$_5$

(ll. 16-19 totally lost)

Rev. 1. [*n*] KUR SA$_5$ *3* KUR *ir-gi-nu*

2. [*n* +] 1 ^{MÍ}ḪÚB KUR PAP *18* KUR^{MEŠ}

3. [*š*]*a* ^{I}*Kur-ba-a-nu*

4. [*n* KUR] GÍG *4* KUR *ir-gi-ni*

5. [*n* KUR] SA$_5$ *15* ^{MÍ}ḪÚB KUR

6. [PAP *n* +]*1* KUR *ša* ^{I}*Ḫa-ba-si*

7. [*n* KUR S]A$_5$ *12* KUR *ir-gi-ni*

8. [*n* ^{MÍ}ḪÚ]B KUR PAP *22* KUR

9. [*ša*] ^{I}*Me-e'-su*

10. [*n* KUR] GÍG^{MEŠ} *1* KUR SA$_5$

11. [*n* ^{MÍ}]ḪÚB KUR PAP *18* KUR

12. [*sa*] ^{I}SUḪUS . XV

(blank space of about three lines)

13. [PAP-*m*]*a* *1 me 64* ⌊ KUR ⌋ [MEŠ]

14. [Š]U^{II} ^{I}DÙ-[*ia* ( )]

Transl.: (*Obv.*) " [ ]? of the palace. [*n* +] 3 *irginu*-colored horses, [ ] *ḫaršāju* horses, six (?) mares, a total of *n* + 1 horses [ ], *n* horses [ ] one horse, [ ], *n* horses, [ ], *n* horses [ ], *n* black horses [ ], .. (1.15:) [*n*] red horses, ...(*Rev.*) *n* red horses, three *irginu*-colored horses, *n* + 1 mares, a total of 18 horses of Kurbānu. *n* black horses, four *irginu*-colored horses, *n* red horses, fifteen mares, a total of *n* + 1 horses of Ḫabasi. *n* red horses, twelve *irginu*-colored horses, *n* mares, a total of 22 horses of Me'su. *n* black horses, one red horse, *n* mares, a total of 18 horses of Išid?-Ištar. A grand total of 164 horses in the hands of Bāniia."

Notes. Obv. 4-15 not copied by Johns (*ADD* II, p. 227).

D. K. 1959 = *ADD* 1103.

*1. [*n*] ⌊ KUR! ⌋ S[A$_5$]^{MEŠ}

2. *2* KUR ⌈ *ḫar-šá* ⌉ *-a-a*

3. [*n* +] *2*! KUR MÍḪÚB^{MEŠ}

4. [PAP] *34* KUR^{MEŠ}

5. [*ša* ^{I}*Aš* + *š*] *ur*!-IGI . LAL-*a-ni*

---

6. [*n* KUR] SA$_5$^{MEŠ}

(remainder lost)

Transl.: "*n* red horses, two *ḫaršāju* horses, *n* + 2 mares, a total of 34 horses of Aššur-ēmuranni. *n* red horses," (remainder lost).

2. The textual group on the color of horses: discussion

Texts A-D presented above are undoubtedly homogeneous under many aspects. On the formal side (i.e., as regards methods of textual composition) all four tablets are concerned with lists of small groups of horses of various types, with each group concluded by a total and a personal name, in A, B and D also by horizontal dividing lines. The occurrence of a second personal name (in all cases = Bāniia), preceded by the expression "in the hands of" (i.e., "at the disposal of", "assigned to", etc.) is rarer, and seems to follow no set rule. In one case (=C, Rev. 13-14), the expression "in the hands of Bāniia" is coupled with the grand total of the horses listed on the tablet, and does not seem to occur elsewhere in the same text. I am aware of the fact that this might be considered an argument in favor of inverting the order of the sides in text B, where a grand total (together with the above-said expression) might be inferred on the lower edge following my "Obverse"; other arguments (especially the relative length of the sections between two dividing lines on the two faces of the text) might, however, be brought up against this view. In any case, the lists on the four tablets are drawn up along virtually identical standards, minor elements of variation consisting in a broader type of section (with one item per line) as opposed to a more tight-knit enumeration (with as many as three items per line in B, Reverse, where the *ditto* sign is used instead of KUR).

As for contents, the terms applied to the horses are for the most part the same in all four documents: this is particularly true of the ideographically written SA$_5$=*sāmu*, "red", GÍG=*ṣalmu*, "black" and ^{MI}ḪÚB=*uritu* (preceded or followed by KUR as the case may be), "mare", and of the syllabically written *ir-gi-nu/-ni,* whereas *ḫar-ša/-šá-a-u* is missing in text A, and *ḫar-ba-ka-nu* occurs only in B, Obv. 11. The order of the terms in the sequences shows many variations but also a few fixed positions, as can be seen from the following chart, in which group totals are also given:

A.

Obv. 1-3:	] -mares	= 6
4 - Lower edge 1:	*irginu*-mares	= 3
Lower edge 2-4:	red-black-mare	= 4
Rev. 1-4:	red-*irginu*-black-mares	= 8
5- :	*irginu*-[	= 1 + *n*

B.

Obv. 1-5:	black-red *irginu*-[(?)] -mares	= 17
6-8:	black-*irginu*-red-mares	= 16
9-14:	*irginu*-red-black-*ḫarbakanu*-*ḫaršāju*-mares	= 26
15-17:	red-*irginu*-black-mares	= 11 + *n*
Rev. 1-3:	black-red-*irginu*-mares	= 5 + *n*
4-6:	red (?)-mares	= 26
7-9:	black-red-*irginu*-[(?)] -mares	= 6 + *n*
10-12:	*irginu*-red (?) - black-mares	= 18
13-15:	red-black-*irginu* (?)-*ḫaršāju*-mares	= 25
16-18:	black (?)- *irginu*-red-*ḫaršāju*-mares	= 17
19-21:	(? = black?)-red-mares	= 18

C.

Obv. 2-4:	[ ] -*irginu*-[ ] -*ḫaršāju*-mares	= 9 + *n*
Rev. 1-3:	red-*irginu*-mares	= 18

4-6: black-*irginu*-red-mares = 19 + *n*

7-9: red-*irginu*-mares = 22

10-12: black-red-mares = 18

D.

1-5:]-red-*ḫaršāju*-mares = 34

6- : red-[= *n*

Lastly, a list of horses is inserted between two parts of a letter or report in text *ABL* 466:[2]

Obv. 6 - Rev. 2: red-*irginu*-black-*ḫaršāju-tu* (?) *anu*[3]-mares.

There seems to be a more or less general agreement on the fact that lists B, C, D and *ABL* 466 are *basically* concerned with colors of horses; cf, most recently, B. Landsberger, *JCS* 21 (1967), 140; A. Salonen, *Hippologica Accadica,* Helsinki 1956, 35; and the dictionaries (*AHw* 240*a*, 324*b*, 328*a*, 857*a; CAD* I/J, 176*b*, Ḫ, 96*b*-97*a*, 115*b*, Ṣ, 77*a*), all of which refer back to K. Balkan, *Die Sprache der Kassiten,* New Haven 1954, 34. Going down to details, no great difficulties are presented by the (consistently) ideographically written terms SA_5 and GÍG, both of which are attested in all complete sequences in the texts presented above (see chart) and occur in Cassite and Nuzian lists of horses as a regular feature (cf. Balkan, *op. cit.*, for an overview).

A greater degree of uncertainty reigns concerning the rendering and the general meaning of *irginu* and *ḫarbakanu* in our lists and elsewhere. For *irginu,* cf. A. Salonen, *loc. cit.*, according to whom the term might derive from **wrq,* " 'grün, gelb sein', mit Endung *-inu*"; but see P. Fronzaroli, *I cavalli del Proto-Zaccaria, RANL* 26 (1971), 595 for the problem of "green" horses in another sector of ancient Near Eastern studies. W. von Soden (*AHw,* 240*a*) considers *irginu* problematically as an "ur(artäisches) F(remd)w(ort)"; while D. J. Wiseman and J. V. Kinnier Wilson (*Iraq* 13 [1951], 111) translate the term as "dun-coloured". My only contribution on the subject stems from the chart given above; as can be seen, the term *irginu* is—when present in complete sequences—placed in 1st, 2nd or 3rd position in five possible sequential relations with "red" and "black" (the latter are consistently among the first three positions):

1 *IRGINU*-RED-BLACK
2 RED-*IRGINU*-BLACK
3 BLACK-*IRGINU*-RED
4 BLACK-RED-*IRGINU*
5 RED-BLACK-*IRGINU*
(*IRGINU*-BLACK-RED not attested)

The close contact between *irginu* and the designations "red" and "black" indicates, in my opinion, that the first three positions in each sequence at least are homogeneous indications of the color of horses; also, that *irginu* is a shade of horses' cloaks as common as the other two. In this light, Wiseman's and Kinnier Wilson's rendering of the term acquires the value of a good working hypothesis, further upheld by the occurrence of red ($SA_5^{MEŠ}$) and *irginu* horses together in text ND 445 (*Iraq* 13,111).

[2] Transliteration of this text in J. N. Postgate, *Taxation and Conscription in the Assyrian Empire,* Rome 1974, p. 279.

[3] My impression of the sign(s) in 1. 10 is -*a-nu*. An interpretation as MU . 2-*a-nu*, although highly problematical, is not to be entirely ruled out, especially in the light of the high degree of uncertainty which surrounds many terms in these lists.

Another Nimrud text might prove useful in clarifying the general meaning of the term *ḫarbak(k)an(n)u*, much less attested in our lists than elsewhere. In list *ND* 446 (*Iraq* 13, 111), a sequence of "black" (GÍG^{MEŠ}), "red" (SA$_5$^{MEŠ}) and ḪAR^{MEŠ} horses is given; the latter term might well be an abbreviation of *ḫarbak(k)an(n)u,* according to a frequent nA use of "cutting" the word at the end of the first syllable. Cf. e.g., *pir* for *pir-su, ku*^{MEŠ} for *ku-dini*^{MEŠ} in plurals, etc., and note that all writings of *ḫarbak(k)an(n)u* present initial *ḫar-*; the abbreviation of a gentilic along the same lines (such as *ḫaršāju,* see further on) strikes me as less frequent and less probable in this context. In any case, other evidence for the association of *ḫarbak(k)an(n)u* with designations of horses' colors is not lacking; in a quite large number of contracts from Nineveh and Nimrud-Kalḫu (cf. *ARU, passim* and especially nos. 162-178; *ADD* 1185, Rev. 15; *ND* 473; 496: Rev. 1-2; 2323; 2324; 2326; 3426:17-19) horses and asses termed *ḫarbakannu/i* are mentioned together with "white horses" (ANŠE.KUR. RA^{MEŠ} BABBAR^{MEŠ}) as offerings to be made to the gods (Aššur, NIN.LÍL, often Nergal, Ištar of Nineveh, Sîn and NIN.GAL of Ḫarrān, Sîn of Dūr-Šarrukīn) by the party breaking the contract. Salonen (*loc. cit.*) merely considers the term as being possibly of Hurrian origin; whereas Wiseman and Kinnier Wilson offer the translation "broken-in asses" for the ANŠE *ḫarbakanni* of one of the Nimrud contracts (*Iraq* 13, 114). I fail to see the plausibility of an opposition between "white" and "broken-in" *equidae* in the context of legal offences and expiatory offerings in temples; on the whole, an opposition between colors—and maybe between a solid shade and a blended one—in the animals' cloaks (the latter type being possibly of less value than the former, as perhaps witnessed by its being always mentioned in second position) seems more probable. This view would certainly not contrast with the position of the *ḫar-ba-ka-nu* horses in B, Obv. 11 above, after *irginu,* red and black; it might even be used to uphold the opinion of *irginu* as being a well-attested (and solid) color in horses' cloaks, therefore formally equivalent to red and black.

The absence of parallel material limits heavily a discussion on the remaining terms in our lists, *ḫaršāju* and *tuanu;* for the rest, these terms flank *irginu* and *ḫarbak(k)an(n)u* in that they offer scarce ground for etymological investigation. The indication *ḫaršāju* (or *ḫaršâ, CAD* Ḫ, 115*b*) is usually considered as connected to a toponym; cf. *CAD* Ḫ, cit., and Salonen, 35, 37-38 for some tentative attributions to place-names. Noteworthy is however the constant absence of determinatives preceding the term, counter to other gentilics denoting types of horses in nA (especially ^{KUR}*Me-sa-a-a,* ^{KUR}*Ku-sa-a-a* in the Nineveh "horse reports"; see p. 17, n.6). For *tuanu,* the only attestation we have is in *ABL* 466, as part of a shipment of horses "of the son of the king of the Andia region" (Rev. 2-3, and cf. Obv. 1-3), possibly connected to *nāmurtu* (Rev. 8) as regards motivation; cf. J. V. Kinnier Wilson, *The Nimrud Wine Lists,* London 1972, 105-106 and J. N. Postgate, *Taxation and Conscription in the Assyrian Empire,* Rome 1974, for surveys of the latter term and its implications.

This being the evidence on hand, we might as well broaden our view so as to encompass the entire range of terms applied to horses in the lists: it will be immediately clear that *ḫaršāju* and *tuanu* represent the end categories in the group of male horses, as set off from the "mares" mentioned in last position in the sequences. We are therefore to deal with a minimum of two oppositions in our lists: the first one concerning the sex of the horses, the second one limited to the first four positions of the male sequence, and concerning the color of the cloak (red, black, *irginu, ḫarbakanu*). The problem of interpreting *ḫaršāju* and *tuanu* may be stated in the following terms: are these two indications to be connected to the latter opposition (and to be ranged among the colors of male horses), or to a third opposition still, possibly related to the age and functionality of the animals? No definite answer can, of course, be given; were there, however, a third opposition in our lists—with *ḫaršāju* and *tuanu* meaning "colts" or the like the difference among colors in the first four positions would have to be understood as functional in distinguishing among male adult horses of equal physical characteristics. In other words, the lists would have been composed with the following categories in mind: (1) male adult horses (*a*: solid colors—red, black, *irginu* in no definite order, *b*: blended colors—*ḫarbakanu*); (2) male non-adult horses (*ḫaršaju, tuanu*); (3) mares. In a different view of the sequences, the age factor would be non-existent, and *ḫaršāju* and *tuanu* would form part of group (1) as male horses, and possibly enter into subgroup (1*b*), the only opposition in the male group being one between solid and blended colors.

A further element of homogeneity in the texts is the presence of Bāniia as recipient of the animals in A, B, and C. We know nothing of his functions; only the broken reference to an *ekallu* in C, Obv. 1 hints to his being an official of the Nineveh administration, charged with receiving the horses brought by others upon their arrival at the palace. Of the shipments themselves, details are also lacking; no dates and no indications of provenience are offered by the texts, although the presence of the same official might again point to a formalized and regular state of affairs, to a well-established bureau with clearly defined functions. In this light, the texts on the colors of horses might possibly form part of a much larger Nineveh archive, connected to a particular section of the administration, the function of which was to collect incoming horses, noting their number and their physical characteristics. It is impossible to say, at the present moment, whether a connection of sorts exists between Bāniia's bureau and other "offices" in the Ninevite administration, charged with viewing and classifying horses in relation to their provenience and use, such as Nabû-šumu-iddina's during the time of Esarhaddon (see below, p. 17 f.).

3. A scribal error.

E. K. 286 = ADD 698.

Obv. 1. *3 me* KUR^{MEŠ} ^{ITU}SIG$_4$ UD *10* KÁM

2. *2 me* *93* KUR^{MEŠ} *4*! GÌR^{MEŠ}

3. PAP *2 me 97*! KUR^{MEŠ} GÌR^{MEŠ}

4. ^{ITU}DU$_6$ UD *8* KÁM

5. PAP *5*! *me 93* KUR^{MEŠ} *4* GÌR^{MEŠ}

6. PAP *5 me 97* KUR GÌR^{MEŠ}

Lower edge 1. *ša* ^{I}*Mu-gal-li*

2. *ša* ^{I}DINGIR-*ú-kal-la-an-ni*

Rev. 1. *na-ṣa-an-ni*

2. PAP! *lim-me* ^{I}*Sa-gab*

3. PAP *5 me 89*! KUR^{MEŠ} *8*! GÌR^{MEŠ}

Transl.: (*Obv.*) "300 horses (arrived) on the 10th of Sīmānu; 293 horses, 4 mules, a total of 297 horses (and) mules, (arrived) on the 8th of Tašrītu: a total of 593 horses, 4 mules (i.e.) 597 horses and mules in all (*lower edge*) of Mugallu, which Ilu-ukallanni (*Rev.*) brought. Total figure for the *limmu* of Sagab: a total of 589 (*sic*) mules".

Notes. No real agreement has ever been reached on the figures of the incoming animals in this text by previous editors and commentators (cf. Peiser, *KB* IV, 148-149, where the final figures were artificially made to be exact, 597 horses and 4 mules, and C. H. W. Johns' copy in *ADD* I, 541, with Rev. 3 reading 587 horses, 14 mules). We are in fact faced with a scribal error in the final calculations, although the total figure 597 is correct, and corresponds to the one in Obv. 6; I daresay the scribe, aware that 597 was the figure to be reached, forgot about having already written once the group totals in Obv. 5, and decided to subtract the mules from the grand total so as to reach the figure for the horses, at this point absent-mindedly considering the 4 mules in Obv. 5 as a second entry in the list and adding them to the 4 mules in Obv. 2. The attained total of 8 mules was therefore subtracted from 597, providing the figure of 589 horses for the two shipments arrived from Tabal in 651 B.C.[4]

4. Two new "horse reports".

F. K. 12045 (=Fig. 4).

Lower edge 1*. ⌜ *18* ⌝ KUR^{MEŠ} ⌜ *ša ni* ⌝ -[*i-ri*]

Reverse 1. *1 me 57* KUR^{MEŠ}

2. *ša pet-ḫal-li*

3. PAP *1 me 75* KUR^{MEŠ}

4. *13* ANŠE *ku-dini*

5. PAP *1 me 88* KUR^{MEŠ} ANŠE *ku-di*[*ni*^{MEŠ}]

6. *u_4-mu an-ni-u*

7. *e-tar-bu-u-ni*

Transl.: (Lower edge): "18 horses 'of the yoke', (Rev.) 157 cavalry horses (and) 13 mules; a total of 188 horses (and) mules have arrived today".

G. 83-1-18, 808 (=Fig. 5).

Obverse 1*. [*n* KUR^{MEŠ}] ⌜ *ša* ⌝ *ni*[*-i-r*]*i*

2. [*la*(?)] *il-li-ku-u-ni* x [x]

3. [PAP] *4 me 78* KUR^{MEŠ} *ša n*[*i-i-ri*]

4. [PAP *n*] KUR *pet*[*-ḫal-li*]

5. [PAP *n*]+5 KUR^{MEŠ} *ku*[*-dini*^{MEŠ}]

6. [*e-tar-bu-u-ni* UD] ⌞ 4? ⌟ K[ÁM]

(remainder lost)

Reverse 1*. x x x x x x

---

[4] ^{I}*Mu-gal-li* should be the king of Tabal named in the Assurbanipal annals, on whom an annual tribute of "stallions" (ANŠE . KUR . RA^{MEŠ} GAL^{MEŠ}) was imposed; see, e.g., *AS* 5 44:80-81. The view that our Mugallu and the king of Tabal are one and the same person is held by M. Streck, *Assurbanipal und die letzten assyrischen Könige* ... , Leipzig 1916, I, p. CCCLI n.3. For the *limmu* of Sagab (651 B.C.), see *RlA* 2, 428; cf. *APN*, 189*b*.

2. [š]*a ni-i-ri* LUGAL *be-lí-ia*

3. [x x *a-*]*ši-bu-ú-tu*

4. [x x x *i-n*]*a lìb-bi*

5. [x x x x x x]*-tu*

6. [x x x x x x] x

(remainder lost)

Transl.: (*Obv.*) "[*n* horses] 'of the yoke' [have not (?)] arrived ... [a total of] 478 horses 'of the yoke', [a total of *n*] cav[alry] horses, [a grand total of *n*] +5 horses and mules [have arrived] on the 4th day (remainder lost). (*Rev.*) .... 'of the yoke', the king my lord [s]taying [in]side [ ] ... [ ] ... " (remainder lost).

The two unpublished fragments given above (F: pinkish clay: 4, 1 x 2, 7 cms.; G: gray clay: 3, 7 x 3, 6 cms.) may be presented alongside a text, which is the product of a join between two well known and separately edited fragments, *ABL* 68 and *ABL* 1450, thus providing us with a virtually complete horse report:

H. K. 1053 (= *ABL* 68) + K. 1533 (= *ABL* 1450) (= Fig. 6).

Obverse. 1. *a-na* LUGAL *be-lí-ia*

2. ÌR-*ka* $^{I.d}$PA.MU.AŠ

3. *lu šùl-mu a-na* LUGAL

4. *be-lí-ia a-dan-niš a-dan-*⌜*niš*⌝

5. ^{d}PA ^{d}AMAR.UD

6. ⌞*a-na*⌟ LUGAL *be-lí-ia*

7. *lik-ru-bu*

8. *8* KUR^{MEŠ} *ša ni-i-ri*

9. *15* KUR *pet*[*-ḫal-li*]

10. PAP *23* [KUR^{MEŠ}]

11. *3* [ANŠE *ku-dini*]

Lower edge 1. *ša* [ ]

2. *3* ANŠE ⌜*ku*⌝-[*dini*]

Reverse 1. *šul-la* [*-me*]

2. PAP 6 ANŠE *ku-di*[*ni*]

3. PAP 29 KUR^{MEŠ} *ku-di* [*ni*$^{\text{(MEŠ)}}$]

4. *ša* ^{URU}*Man-ṣu-a-te*

5. ⌊ *u*$_4$*-mu* ⌋ *an-ni-ú*

6. *e-tar-bu-u-*⌈ *ni* ⌉

7. ^{ITU}GU$_4$ UD 7 KÁM

Transl.: (*Obv.*) "To the king my lord, your servant Nabû-šumu-iddina; good health to the king my lord. May the gods Nabû and Marduk very much bless the king my lord. Eight horses 'of the yoke', fifteen cavalry horses, a total of 23 horses; 3 mules (*lower edge*) of [ ]; 3 mules of the type (?) (*Rev.*) *šullame,* a total of six mules; a grand total of 29 horses and mules of the town Manṣuate have arrived today, the 7th of Aiaru".

5. On horse reports: time and other matters.

Texts F and G, and H in its present form, constitute additional material to the textual category of the Nineveh "horse reports", studied by J. N. Postgate as part of his *Taxation and Conscription in the Assyrian Empire* (Rome 1974; esp. pp. 7-18). These documents certainly shed a great deal of information on the provenience of the horses which arrived at the offices of the Assyrian central administration, on their quantities and types; all this information has been very extensively collected by Postgate, and need hardly be taken up again.[5] But the same texts are also interesting as examples of bureaucratic procedures in the Assyrian court; this side of the matter seems well worth examining, as it can, in my opinion, yield something about the workings of the administration at Nineveh in Sargonid times.

As some of the problems involved hinge upon the nature of the "horse reports", I quote Postgate on the subject: "I have so named [*i.e.* "horse reports"] a group of letters from the Kouyunjik archive, which are reports (mostly written by one person) of the numbers and types of horses (and mules) received daily by his department" (p.7), and in a footnote to the above: "There are of course other letters from the Kouyunjik archive which deal with horses, often listing their numbers and varieties (e.g. colours); but my concern here is only with the one group of texts forming an archive." I believe that the view on the horse reports' forming a single and separate archive in themselves can only represent an outcome of investigation, not so much a starting point for it; in any case, an archive seems to differ from a mere *group* of texts in that the documents are kept together in one spot, are felt to be a record of one particular aspect of administration, and may be referred to, long after their having been written, as sources of information on that aspect. Now, this is not the case of the Nineveh horse reports in my opinion.

In this connection, the way the time factor was noted in the reports seems important. As a category, the texts may be termed lists of horses and mules presented according to the basic standards of nA letter-writing, and comprise (a) greeting formulae, (b) the list itself – one long sentence, with a fixed structure which may be formalized[6] – and (c) possibly a *post scriptum*, which always refers (when present) to measures to be taken

[5] See the Excursus at the end of this article.

[6] As follows: (1) number of the animals, (2) type, in a broad sense (KUR/ANŠE.KUR.RA or ANŠE), (3) type, in a more specific sense (*ša nīri,* (*ša*) *petḫalli, kudīni,* and the three sub-groups of *ša nīri:* ^{KUR}*Ku-sa-a-a, ṣibte ša* ^{KUR}*Ku-sa-a-a,* ^{KUR}*Me-sa-a-a*), (4) indications of provenience, sometimes preceded by partial sums, (5) "extra notes" on the shipments, sometimes present (e.g. *la gammarūni*), (6) grand total, often preceded by an overall recount of the animals according to type, i.e., according to (2) and (3), (7) date (relative–"today"–sometimes also absolute–day and month), in connection with the verb *erābu* (seldom *qarābu* and *alāku*), "to come, enter, arrive", which concludes the sentence beginning with (1).

as regards the animals after their arrival. The main indications of time are at the end of the list of incoming animals: the date is always noted as *ūmu annīu*, "today," much less frequently coupled with an absolute notation (day and month). The latter, not being always present, is clearly a secondary feature in the texts; it may uphold, but not act as a substitute for, the basic belief that the document was written "today," common to the writer Nabû-šumu-iddina/Nadinu and to the king, who received the text. It follows that the text had a function limited to the time-span of one day; also, a basic date of the relative type such as "today" could not allow one to keep a systematically ordered archive of the horse reports. While not being destroyed, they were probably discarded after having been read, if they were read at all day after day; a reductive attitude to take toward these texts would be to view their basic function as that of being sent on one hand, simply received on the other, during the time-span of one day (see above, p. 14).

The *post scriptums* to the lists (defined above) provide us with a similar picture of temporal relativity, and of scarce interest for the punctual aspect of time, as do the lists themselves: the terms used here are "yesterday," "tonight," "early tomorrow morning," and regard operations to be undertaken before, or after, the different "todays." One would expect, at this point, the operations themselves to be always different, based on a "day-by-day" standard of military-bureaucratic procedure; but this is not so. If we scan these *post scriptums,* we find a record of repeated measures, instructions, demands for orders; e.g. in the following assurances, given by the writer, that he will set the horses in order: [*n*] ⌜ANŠE-KUR-RA⌝ ^{MEŠ} / . . . / *ina kal-la-ma-a-ri* / *a-sa-di-ir* (*ABL* 71, 17, Rev. 6-7); KUR^{MEŠ} *as-si-dir* and KUR^{MEŠ} *la-as-dir* (*ABL* 371, Rev. 8, 12); *ina kal-la-ma-ri* / ANŠE . KUR . RA^{MEŠ} / *a-sa-di-ir* (*ABL* 375, 12-14); (the horses) *la-as-de-e-ri* / *ina ši-a-ri* (*ABL* 440, 14-Rev. 1); *ina kal-la-ma-a-ri* ANŠE . KUR . RA^{MEŠ} / *la-as-de-e-ri* (*ABL* 545, Rev. 9-10), "tonight / early tomorrow morning I shall set the horses in order." This operation is tightly connected to the consent of the king; it shall be done "according to what the king shall tell me/write me/want me to do" (see *ABL* 71, Rev. 11-13; 371, Rev. 11-14; 375, 12-Rev. 1; 440, 14-Rev. 4; 545, Rev. 9-13). We may well ask ourselves, in this context, if it was really necessary for the king to provide every time Nabû-šumu-iddina with an answer which must have been as stereotype as the request; I only know of cases in which the king writes to ask for missing data – cases which might therefore be considered a bit out of the ordinary procedure, and even then, it is only to ask a fixed question, to which Nabû-šumu-iddina gives a fixed answer. Cf. *ABL* 428, Rev. 1-3, in which the king enquires after a particular shipment ^{LÚ}*2-u* / *ša* ^{LÚ}*tur-tan-ni* / *e-tar-ba-a* ("has the 'second' of the *turtanu* arrived?"), and *ABL* 1153, Rev. 3, regarding some horses, *te-tar-ba*[*-a*] ("have they arrived?"), and the official's answer, in both cases negative (*ABL* 428, Rev. 4-5: *ú-di-i-ni* / *la e-ra-ba; ABL* 1153, Rev. 4-5: *ú-di-i*[*-ni*] / *la te-ra*[*-ba*], "it/they has/have not yet arrived"). Standard though these formulae may seem, they refer to somewhat exceptional cases, for normally Nabû-šumu-iddina /Nadinu makes a point of stating clearly in his lists who (being expected) has not arrived, and who has, and in what conditions: see Postgate's chart (pp. 8-9) and footnotes (p. 10) for the formulae *gammarūni, la gammarūni,* ^{LÚ}*šaniūte la erabūni,* and *e-tar-bu-u-ni la gam-ma-ru-ni* (in No. 6 = *ABL* 71, twice), to which data from *ABL* 1159 should be added, concerning 58 horses ^{KUR}*Ku-sa-a-a,* 24 of which *TA ^{LÚ}*rak-su-ti it-tal-ku-u-ni* (cf. J. V. Kinnier Wilson, *The Nimrud Wine Lists,* 59), whereas of two more groups it is said, respectively, that *la i*[*l*] - ⌜*lak*⌝ - [*u-ni*] and *u-di-*[*ni*] *la il-lak-u-ni;* see also text H, above.

The "image" of these texts (i.e. their formal character as evidence in understanding the bureaucratic context in which they are to be fitted) seems therefore to be defined by two series of facts, apparently disconnected, in fact merging into a single framework. On the one hand, there is a general vagueness about time – hardly modified by a few absolute dates – both in the lists of animals and in the *post scriptums;* on the other hand, the lists present a totally standard form of composition, and the *post scriptums* (which we would expect to display the problems posed by the shipments in an informal fashion) seem, for the most part, to be conceived along ready-made lines and questionnaires. This dualism between imprecision in time-reckoning and precision in operations can be extended to other aspects of the horse reports: again relativism in time ("today") has unerring time-reckoning as its counterpart (the delivery of the text is always made on the day of its composition); a statement of originality in time ("tomorrow morning I shall set the horses in order") reflects in fact permanence in time (illuminating in this respect is the use of the adverb *kajjamānīu,* "continuously", in the *post scriptums,* cf. *ABL* 71, Rev. 9, *ABL* 371, Rev. 9); limited functionality of the texts in time (tablets read and discarded) corresponds to temporal regularity in the composition (after each arrival, and perhaps every day).

How are we to define documents presenting this combination of characteristics? The term which comes to mind (although the aim is not to find a term, but a historical framework) is "memorandum", in its use in modern bureaucratic contexts: a report which is usually sent to a superior, and which constitutes a clear summary of a certain amount of paperwork done by subordinates. These memorandums are written with the aim of keeping the superior informed on new facts and recent developments; they need not necessarily be kept in archives officially, since they are "for internal use". They are required of the lower in rank; they are to be received by the superior, not necessarily read by him; but in case they were, it is good policy to make a show of engaging the man in the subordinates' problems, asking for advice, etc., although nothing new may have intervened from the previous memorandum. The Assyrian horse reports, all considered, seem to fit in a similar bureaucratic context; beneath the clear style in which the subject-matter is put forth, I believe we should imagine the presence of many separate administrative tablets, recording incoming groups of animals, written each day by the Nineveh bureau to which this function was assigned. When this task was over, and before beginning the (night-time or early morning) operations of dividing, ordering and allotting the horses, a brief report was written, informing the king in clear terms on how things had gone during the day, and reminding him (through a formal request for consent) of which measures were to be taken next. This is the type of text, of which some examples have come down to us; whereas the former type – the preliminary administrative tablet – might even, as far as we know, correspond to the documents persented at the beginning of this article.

6. Excursus.

I take this opportunity to provide a few remarks on the chart and commentary published by J. N. Postgate, *Taxation and Conscription in the Assyrian Empire* (Rome 1974, pp. 7-18). My remarks derive from a brief examination of the texts made in the light of the present work in April 1973.

No. 3 = *ABL* 376: I agree on *Dim-maš*$^{!}$*-qa*$^{!}$; Parpola, *Toponyms*, 357:4/III to be corrected accordingly.

No. 6 = *ABL* 684 (footnote on p. 10): the second total might, of course, refer to a previous shipment of 245 horses, which had arrived on the same day and had already been the object of one of Nabû-šumu-iddina's reports. The report we have would, in this light, refer to a second arrival later in the day, unexpected as such, which forced the official to "reopen his registers" for the day 23; it will be noticed that in no. 7 = *ABL* 371 the hardly legible figures for riding-horses ([*n* KUR^{MEŠ}] *ša pet-ḫal-li* / [*n* KUR^{MEŠ} *ša*] *pet-ḫal-li* in Obv. 19 / Rev. 2) also refer to the 23rd day.

No. 9 = *ABL* 538: ^{URU}[*Gu*]-⌞*za*$^{!}$⌟-*na* was my impression of the first toponym in the list; this place-name is coupled with that of ^{URU}*Si-i'-me-e* in no. 25.

No. 11 = *ABL* 63: see now also *CAD* K, 491*b* for the emendation 17$^{!}$.

No. 12 = *ABL* 61: agreeing with Postgate, Rev. 7ff. might be read as follows: ^{7}PAP 98 ⌜ANŠE$^{!}$⌝.KUR.⌜RA$^{!}$⌝ M[EŠ] ^{8}*š*[*u ni-i-ri*] ^{9}⌜*u*$_4$$^{!}$⌝-[*mu an-ni-u*] ^{10}*e*$^{!}$-[*tar-bu-*]*u*$^{!}$*-n*[*i*]. The two remaining lines might represent a brief *post scriptum* to the list, regarding measures to be taken after the arrival of the horses, as in *ABL* 71, 371, 373, 375, 545, 575, 1017: a horizontal wedge marks the beginning of line 11, whereas *u-sa-*[opens line 12, the last on the tablet.

No. 14 = *ABL* 1379: notice PAP$^{!}$ ^{URU}BÀD.MAN-*uk-ka* in l. 11, a variant to the usual *ša* + SOURCE formation. In P.'s reconstruction of the figures of this much-worn text, the totals certainly correspond to the sum of the single items, but collations and emendations could have been noted at least for the less legible and more problematical points: e.g., in l. 12 the numeral is entirely gone and can only be reconstructed from Rev. 3; the 3 mules of l. 14 are a (correct) reconstruction from Rev. 6, the tablet bearing [*n* +] 1 in the former passage.

No. 15 = *ABL* 1450: see now text H, above.

No. 20 = *ABL* 395: my reading of the second toponym confirms (with a slight correction) Parpola, *Toponyms,* 140:5, ^{URU}*Ḫa-da-*[x]*-a-il.* The figures for Arpadda seemed problematical both on the *ša nīri* and on the *petḫalli* side: I saw  ,40 [+ *n* ?] and  ⌜66$^{?}$⌝ / ⌜69$^{?}$⌝.

No. 23 = *ABL* 601: P.'s second position total for *ša nīri,* 49$^{!}$, is of course a consequence of his reading of the figure for the *ṣi-ib-te ša* ^{KUR}*Ku-sa-a-a* as 17, in lieu of 7 (*ABL, RCAE*); cf., however, other figures for the category in the same text and in no. 2.

No. 24 = *ABL* 649: the interpretation of the sentence beginning with *5 ú-ra-a-te* (11. 6-10; see P. 's footnote on p. 10) presents undoubtedly not a few difficulties. Cf. *CAD* Ṣ, 182*b* and B, 68*a* for quotations of single lines (1.7 and 1.9, respectively); for the latter, my reading was slightly more explicit:  [( )] *ina*$^{!}$ *bat*$^{!}$*-ta-ta-a-a* etc. We lack the relative sentence on which *ipqidanni* depends and the subject of the action in the verb: hypothetically, "which the *turtanu* 'of the left' "-the ideal position of which would be after 1.8-might be considered the logical subject of the sentence. For *ḫi-se-te* see perhaps *ḫissatu,* "mention, reference", also keeping in mind a further letter on horses, probably by Nabû-šumu-iddina himself, *ABL* 1153 (kindly brought to my attention by Prof. K. Deller and Dr. S. Parpola; collations by the latter). The king has been asking about the arrival of a particular group of horses; the official can only answer him that, as regards the horses (1.8: *ina* UGU *ú-r*[*a*$^{?}$*-ta*/*a-te*?), "they have not yet arrived" (see p. 14, above), and adds (Rev., 11.6-10) ^{6}*mi-i-nu* ^{7}TA* *pa-an ḫi-s*[*e-te*] ^{8}*ša* LUGAL *be-lí*[*-ia*] ^{9}*lu-la-a* x [x(x)] ^{10}É *pa-aq-* x [x] , perhaps "for what reason should I remove them from a mention for (*lit.*, 'of') the king my lord, when they have been assign[ed to me] ?". In the case of No. 24, the object should be an "already mentioned" (*lit.* of mention') shipment, of which the five horses *ša ṣeḫrūte* " < which the *turtanu* 'of the left' > in periods of time one following the other has assigned to me" form part.

p. 11, *ad* 6.4 (= *ABL* 575, Rev. 6): I should read here ^{4}ANŠE . KUR . RA^{MEŠ} ^{5}*ša ina* ŠÀ É.GAL ^{6}*ša a-na ra*$^{!}$*-ku-si* ^{7}*ša* LUGAL *be-lí ṭè-e-mu* ^{8}*iš-ku-na-ni-ni* (11.9 and 10 almost totally lost); the passage would therefore represent another case for the discussion, opened by Postgate (p. 12 and note 1), on the meaning of *rakkusu* in the horse reports, with no bearing on the question of the ^{KUR}*Ku-sa-a-a* horses.

Obv. *1

4

Lower edge 1

Rev. 1

5

Fig. 1
(Rm. 949)

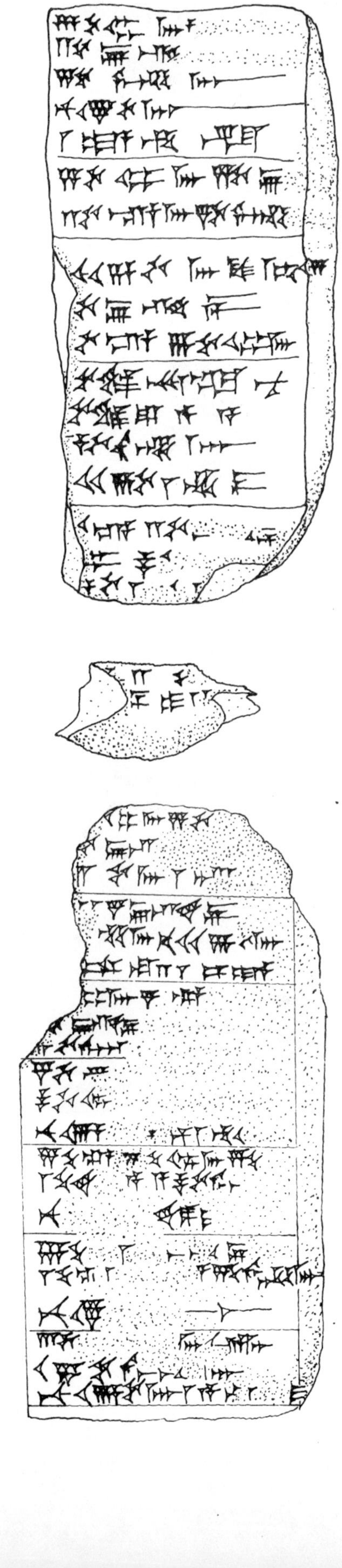

Fig. 2
(K. 952 = *ADD* 988)

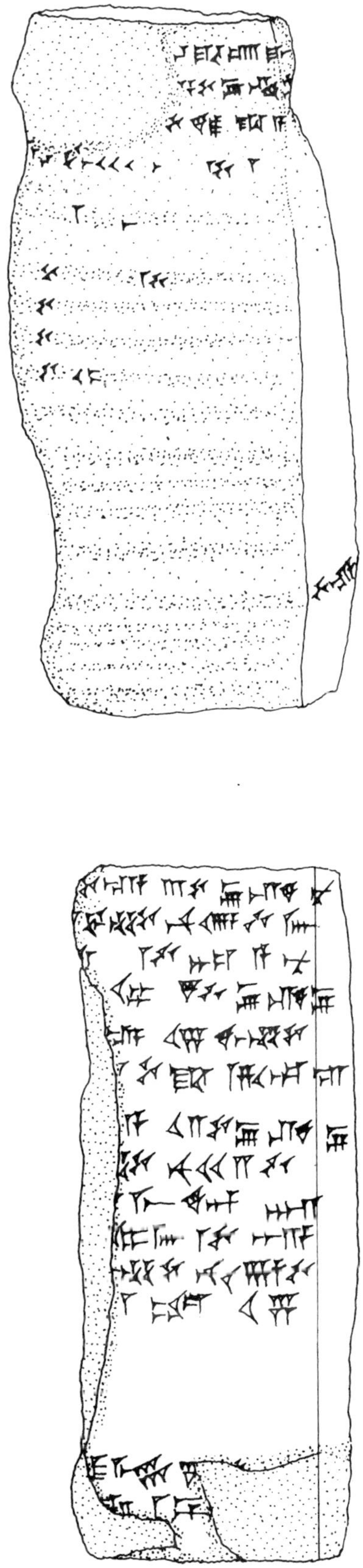

Fig. 3
(K 968 = *ADD* 989)

Lower edge 1

Rev. 1

Fig. 4
(K. 12045)

Obv. *1

Rev. *1

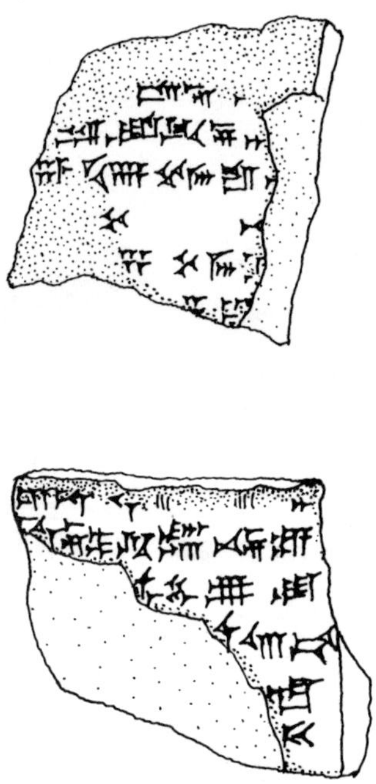

Fig. 5
(83-1-18, 808)

Obv. *1

Lower edge 1

Rev. 1

Fig. 6
(K. 1053 = *ABL* 68
+ K. 1533 = *ABL* 1450)

MONOGRAPHIC JOURNALS OF THE NEAR EAST

General Editor: Giorgio Buccellati

MJNE is a system of journals on the Near East, with each journal devoted to a specialized study area, and each issue consisting of a single article.

General Subscription

For a prepayment of $10 the subscriber selects random issues from within the entire system as desired, up to a total of 200 pages. The subscriber is also entitled to (1) periodical lists of abstracts from all journals in the system, and (2) reservation to any journal within the system, whereby issues of a given journal are sent on approval immediately upon publication (and may be returned within two weeks).

Library Subscription

A prepayment of $10 for each journal in the system secures all issues of a single volume as soon as they are published. This subscription schedule does not allow the selection of random issues; in return, a discount is provided in the form of a greater number of pages for the basic price of $10 (since a volume will normally include more than 200 pages).

Payment must accompany orders from individuals. A handling fee of 70¢ will be charged to Libraries if order is not prepaid. Order from: UNDENA PUBLICATIONS, P.O.Box 97, Malibu, California 90265, U.S.A.

AFROASIATIC LINGUISTICS

AAL includes contributions in linguistics within the vast domain of Afroasiatic (Hamito-Semitic) languages. Articles of general, theoretical interest using Afroasiatic material, descriptive, historical and comparative studies are included.

Editor: Robert Hetzron (1346 San Rafael, Santa Barbara, Ca. 93109 U.S.A.)
Advisory Board: A. Ambros, A. Bloch, J. B. Callender, T. Givón, T. G. Penchoen, S. Segert

Volume 1

Issue 1: P. Newman & R. G. Schuh, *The Hausa Aspect System*, 38 pp.

In this paper the authors hope to account for the aspect marking constructions of modern Hausa by providing detailed historical explanations of their origin and development, beginning with morphological forms and syntactic patterns reconstructed for Proto-Hausa. The description accounts for the asymmetry in certain paradigms, the lack of parallelism between affirmative and negative paradigms in certain aspects, and some of the differences between contemporary dialects. The hypotheses about Hausa history are supported by reliable comparative data from other Chadic languages.

Issue 2: J. L. Malone, *The Development of the Anomalous Syriac Verb eškāh 'To Find': A Case of Convergent Factors in Linguistic Change*, 10 pp.

The canonically anomalous shape of the Syriac Verb *eškáh* 'to find' is shown to result from a convergence of diachronic pressures on an intersection of phonological weak spots and morpho-syntactic defectiveness for moderate phonological anomaly. The developmental hypothesis adopted underscores the importance both of multiple factors in diachronic change and of homeostasis in linguistic systems.

Issue 3: R. Hetzron, *Extrinsic Ordering in Classical Arabic*, 25 pp.

One speaks of extrinsic ordering when the order of application of two rules must be specifically indicated and does not follow from a general principle. In Arabic the survival of a long vowel in a syllable made closed by a contraction may be a case of such ordering, though it may also be interpreted as an intrinsically ordered sequel of 'nonproductive–operative' rules. On the other hand, the incongruent agreement of numerals with the underlying singulars of the co-occurring plural nouns is definitely extrinsically ordered.

SOURCES AND MONOGRAPHS ON THE ANCIENT NEAR EAST

Editor: Giorgio Buccellati

These two series make available original documents in English translation (Sources) and important studies by modern scholars (Monographs) as a contribution to the study of history, religion, literature, art and archaeology of the Ancient Near East. Inexpensive and flexible in format, they are meant to serve the specialist by bringing within easy reach basic publications often in updated versions, to provide imaginative educational outlets for undergraduate and graduate courses, and to reach the interested segments of the educated lay audience.

Each fascicle is issued separately as part of a volume. One may either purchase single fascicles or subscribe to entire volumes.

The subscription price is $8 per volume. A volume will average 200 pages. Periodicity in the order of appearance of fascicles is not predetermined, but a volume will normally be completed within one year.

Payment must accompany orders from individuals. A handling fee of 70¢ will be charged to Libraries if order is not prepaid.

Order from: UNDENA PUBLICATIONS, P.O.Box 97, Malibu, California 90265, U. S. A.

SOURCES FROM THE ANCIENT NEAR EAST

Volume 1

Fascicle 1: R. I. Caplice, *The Akkadian Namburbi Texts: An Introduction*
24 pp., 80¢

Namburbi is the title of a group of typical Babylonian incantations, used to "undo" or avert portended evil. Consisting of both rituals and prayers, they provide a response to the observed events taken by the Mesopotamians to be signs of future happenings; thus they are the practical correlate of the "omen texts," which list such portents and their significance. The fascicle by Caplice includes a long introduction, which explains the nature of the texts and their ritual *Sitz im Leben,* and the translation, with notes, of 14 representative texts, ranging from a Ritual for the Evil of a Snake to a Ritual to Secure Brisk Trade.

MONOGRAPHS ON THE ANCIENT NEAR EAST

Volume 1

Fascicle 1: A. Falkenstein, *The Sumerian Temple City* (1954)
Introduction and Translation by M. deJ. Ellis, 21 pp. 75¢

An important article which first appeared in 1954 in a French version published in the journal *Cahiers d'Histoire Mondiale*. The present version has been done directly from the German original, provided specifically by the author for the purposes of this series. Focusing on two major dimensions of one of the earliest historical civilizations, i.e. the urban and the religious dimensions, the fascicle describes in detail, and with reference to primary sources, the organization of the temple and its interrelationship with the political and social order of ancient Sumer.

Fascicle 2: B. Landsberger, *Three Essays on the Sumerians* (1943-45)
Introduction and Translation by M. deJ. Ellis, 18 pp. 70¢

This series of articles appeared during the Second World War in a Turkish journal, in a dual German and Turkish version–and as a result they have not enjoyed the diffusion which their importance would have warranted. They represent one of the rare attempts of that giant of Assyriological studies, Benno Landsberger, at presenting a synthesis of his views on Sumerian culture; in this sense, they constitute a classical and comprehensive formulation, which has lost none of its original vigor and freshness. The translation, based on the German text, was still revised by the author before his death.

Fascicle 3: I. M. Diakonoff, *Structure of Society and State in Early Dynastic Sumer* (1959)
Summary and translation of selected passages by the author
Introduction by M. Desrochers, 16 pp., 50¢

The article presented here appeared as the English resumé to I.M.Diakonoff's *Sumer: State and Society in Ancient Mesopotamia,* Moscow 1959. This book's publication marked a turning point in Assyriological studies, for, as the first exposé of the Russian school of Assyriology to become widely known in the West, it opened the way for future meaningful exchanges between Western and Soviet Assyriologists. I.M.Diakonoff stands at the head of two generations of Soviet Assyriologists, a major portion of the second generation having studied under him at the University of Leningrad. The introduction provides a review of the major contributions by Diakonoff available in western languages.